BLESSED NAMES

BLESSED NAMES 12

WHY WAS HE NAMED AL-HADI (A)?

WRITTEN BY:
KISA KIDS PUBLICATIONS

Please recite a Fātiḥah for the marḥūmīn
of the Rangwala family, the sponsors of this book.

All proceeds from the sale of this book
will be used to produce more educational resources.

Dedication

This book is dedicated to the beloved Imām of our time (AJ). May Allāh (swt) hasten his reappearance and help us to become his true companions.

Acknowledgements

Prophet Muḥammad (s): The pen of a writer is mightier than the blood of a martyr.

True reward lies with Allāh, but we would like to sincerely thank Shaykh Salim Yusufali and Sisters Sabika Mithani, Liliana Villalvazo, Zahra Sabur, Kisae Nazar, Sarah Assaf, Nadia Dossani, Fatima Hussain, Naseem Rangwala, and Zehra Abbas. We would especially like to thank Nainava Publications for their contributions. May Allāh bless them in this world and the next.

Preface

Prophet Muḥammad (s): Nurture and raise your children in the best way. Raise them with the love of the Prophet and the Ahl al-Bayt (a).

Literature is an influential form of media that often shapes the thoughts and views of an entire generation. Therefore, in order to establish an Islamic foundation for the future generations, there is a dire need for compelling Islamic literature. Over the past several years, this need has become increasingly prevalent throughout Islamic centers and schools everywhere. Due to the growing dissonance between parents, children, society, and the teachings of Islam and the Ahl al-Bayt (a), this need has become even more pressing. Al-Kisa Foundation, along with its subsidiary, Kisa Kids Publications, was conceived in an effort to help bridge this gap with the guidance of ʿulamah and the help of educators. We would like to make this a communal effort and platform. Therefore, we sincerely welcome constructive feedback and help in any capacity.

The goal of the *Blessed Names* series is to help children form a lasting bond with the 14 Māʿṣūmīn by learning about and connecting with their names. We hope that you and your children enjoy these books and use them as a means to achieve this goal, inshā'Allāh. We pray to Allāh to give us the strength and tawfīq to perform our duties and responsibilities.

With Duʾās,
Nabi R. Mir (Abidi)

Kisa Kids Publications
4415 Fortran Court
San Jose, CA 95134
(260) KISA-KID [547-2543]

An Introduction to the Blessed Names

Our names are a very special part of us. Many times, they shape our personalities and even explain who we are or the person we would like to become. In this series, you will explore the names and titles of our beloved 14 Ma'soomeen. Did you know that their names and titles were not just ordinary names? They were special because they were given to them by Allah!

Allah has given seven special heavenly names to our Ma'soomeen: Muhammad, Ali, Fatimah, Hasan, Husain, Ja'far, and Musa. Behind each of these names is a heavenly power!

In addition to their names, each of the Ma'soomeen also had special titles by which they became famous. Their titles were often given to them because of the circumstances of their time, but these titles and characteristics were common amongst all the Ma'soomeen. For example, Imam al-Baqir (a) was known for spreading knowledge because he was able to create many new universities and branches of knowledge during his time. However, if the other Ma'soomeen had the same opportunity, they, too, would have spread knowledge and created universities in their teaching circles. In these stories, you will discover some of the reasons why the Ma'soomeen received their specific names or titles.

Many of us share our names with these beloved Ma'soomeen or know people who do. Let's learn about these blessed names and titles so we can strive to be like our blessed Ma'soomeen!

I think al-Hadi means...

The large caliph sat on his grand throne, drinking from a goblet of wine. Soldiers in matching uniforms surrounded him, guarding his palace.

The caliph's trusted vizier, a corrupt man, leaned in and whispered into his ear, "Mutawakkil, my master, I have heard that there are weapons and money — lots of money — in Imam al-Hadi's house! He is definitely planning something against you!"

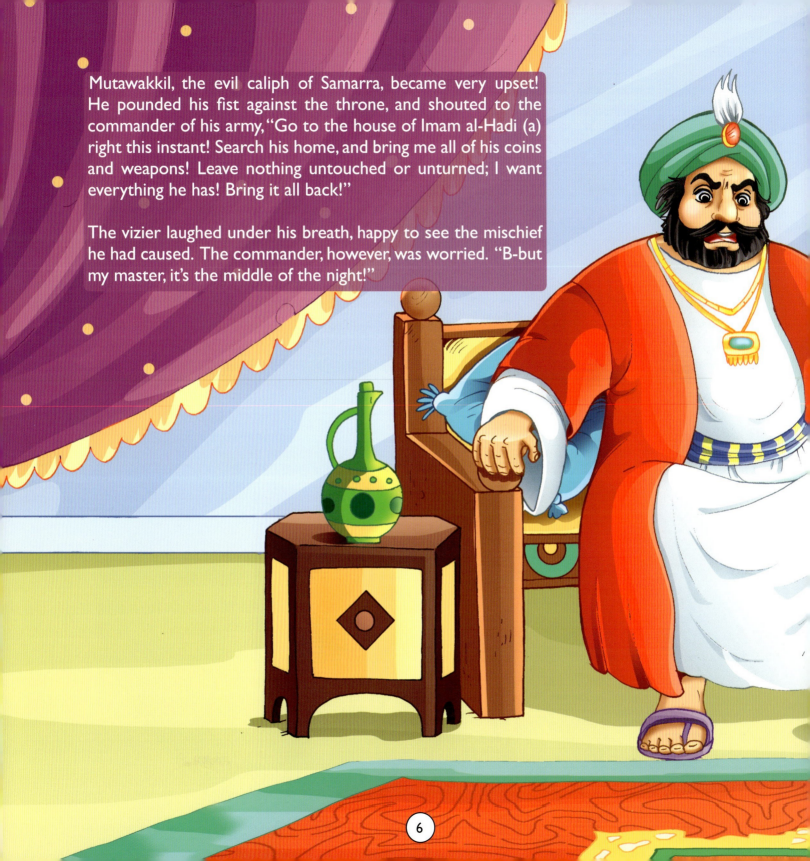

Mutawakkil, the evil caliph of Samarra, became very upset! He pounded his fist against the throne, and shouted to the commander of his army, "Go to the house of Imam al-Hadi (a) right this instant! Search his home, and bring me all of his coins and weapons! Leave nothing untouched or unturned; I want everything he has! Bring it all back!"

The vizier laughed under his breath, happy to see the mischief he had caused. The commander, however, was worried. "B-but my master, it's the middle of the night!"

Mutawakkil replied, "Don't you dare question me! Do as I say! Go now!" The commander and his soldiers bowed and left to search the Imam's house and capture him.

Mutawakkil returned to his throne and murmured, "He is trying to keep money from *me*? Ha! We'll see about that!" He then tipped back his goblet and took a big gulp.

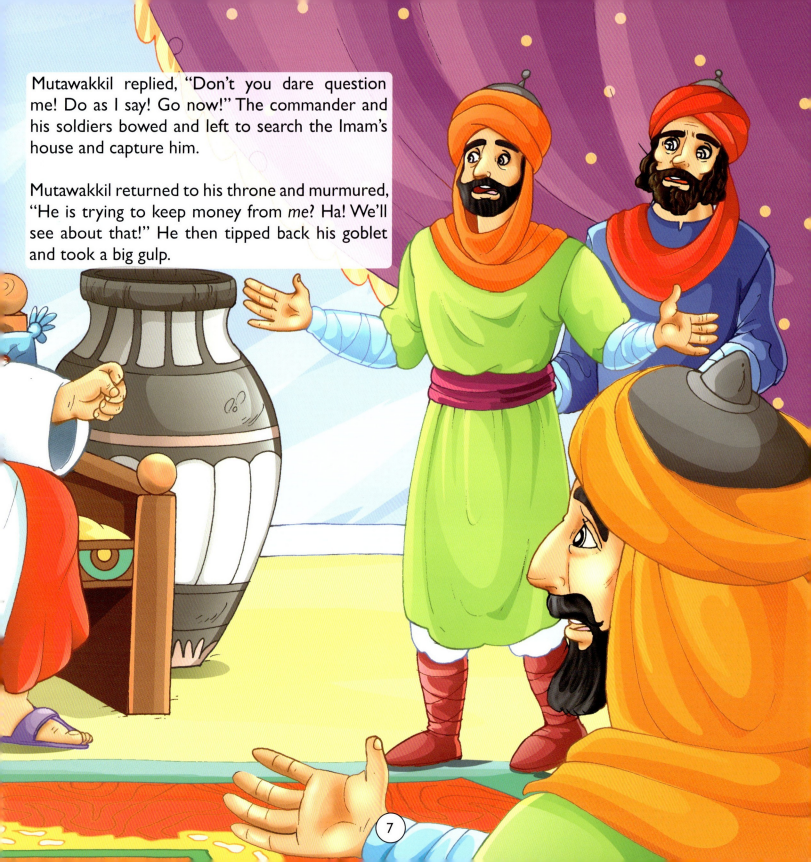

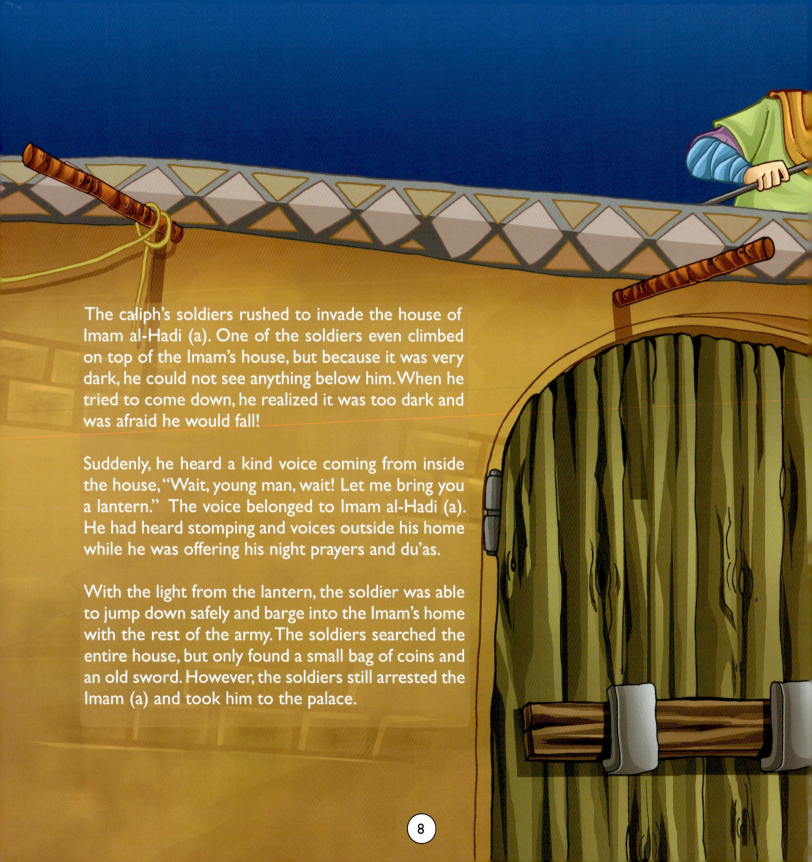

The caliph's soldiers rushed to invade the house of Imam al-Hadi (a). One of the soldiers even climbed on top of the Imam's house, but because it was very dark, he could not see anything below him. When he tried to come down, he realized it was too dark and was afraid he would fall!

Suddenly, he heard a kind voice coming from inside the house, "Wait, young man, wait! Let me bring you a lantern." The voice belonged to Imam al-Hadi (a). He had heard stomping and voices outside his home while he was offering his night prayers and du'as.

With the light from the lantern, the soldier was able to jump down safely and barge into the Imam's home with the rest of the army. The soldiers searched the entire house, but only found a small bag of coins and an old sword. However, the soldiers still arrested the Imam (a) and took him to the palace.

9

Back in the palace, the vizier was laughing, happy to see Imam al-Hadi (a) arrested. The commander came forward and handed Mutawakkil the old sword and bag of coins.

"My master, this is all we found" he said.

When his eyes fell on the bag of coins, the caliph noticed a familiar stamp on it. It was the special stamp that belonged to his mother. He turned towards the Imam (a) and demanded, "Where did you get these coins from?! This bag belongs to my mother! Did you steal this from her?!"

Mutawakkil ordered that his mother be brought to the court immediately, even though it was the middle of the night.

When Mutawakkil's mother entered the court, he immediately asked her why Imam al-Hadi (a) had her coins. She softly replied, "Remember that time when you were very sick? I made a promise to Allah that if you got better, I would give 10,000 gold coins to the Imam (a). Alhamdulillah, you got better, and I gave Imam al-Hadi (a) the coins as promised."

By now, Mutawakkil had become very angry! He turned to his vizier and whispered, "You told me he had gathered lots of money and weapons to use against me! What happened?! Where are they?" The vizier hung his head in shame and embarrassment.

The caliph didn't want to show that he was defeated. He quickly drank the rest of his wine and filled up his cup again. He rose from his throne and stumbled towards the Imam (a).

He chuckled and handed him his wine glass, "Here, drink this! I invite you to stay and join my party. Have fun and be happy just like the rest of us!"

The Imam (a) was very upset by the caliph's actions. He firmly replied, "Never! I swear by Allah that my entire body, even my flesh and blood, find alcohol disgusting."

Upon hearing these words, Mutawakkil's face turned red. He tried embarrassing the Imam (a) again by teasing him. In a mocking voice, he said, "Okay, if you do not want to drink, then why don't you sing for us instead?"

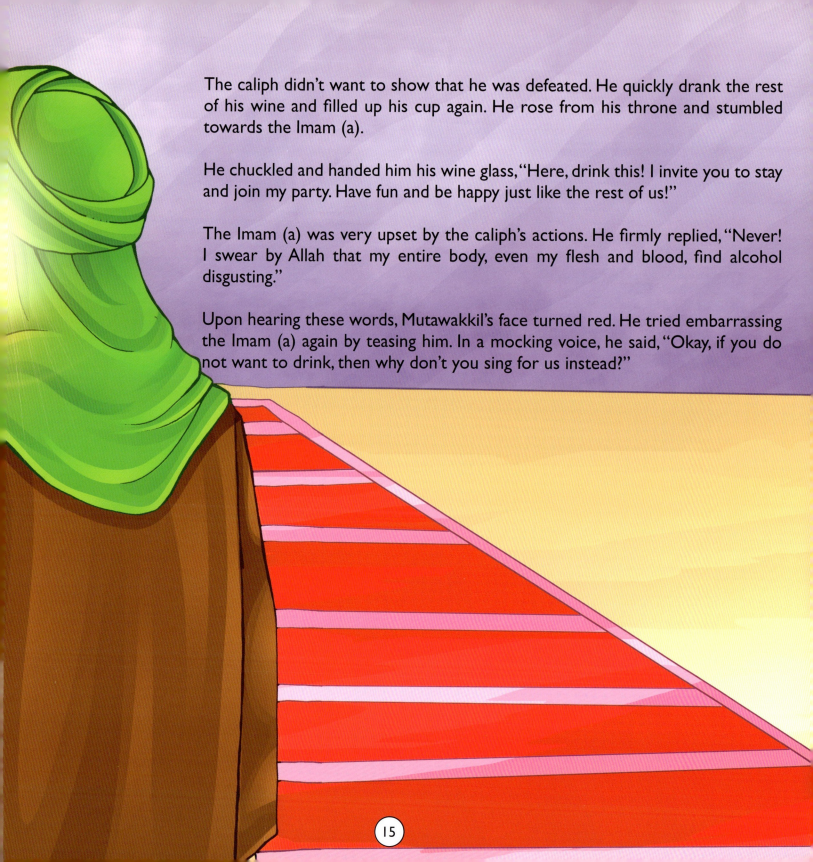

When the Imam (a) did not respond, Mutwakkil continued taunting him, "Come on, what's the problem? Let's hear it now!" The Imam (a) looked around and noticed that everyone around him was drinking wine and laughing. He felt sad seeing this kind of behavior from people who called themselves Muslims. Finally, he said, "Believers do not sing the type of songs that you like to hear, but I will recite a poem instead to remind you of Allah, your Creator."

The Imam (a) began reciting, "*They build forts on top of mountains; strong men guard these forts, but there is no point. Their power and greatness will soon disappear. In the end, they will all die and fall into their graves. When they are buried, voices will call out, 'Now where are your palaces and crowns? Where are the castles and forts to protect you now?' How long they ate and drank! But after eating for so long, they themselves were...eaten!*"

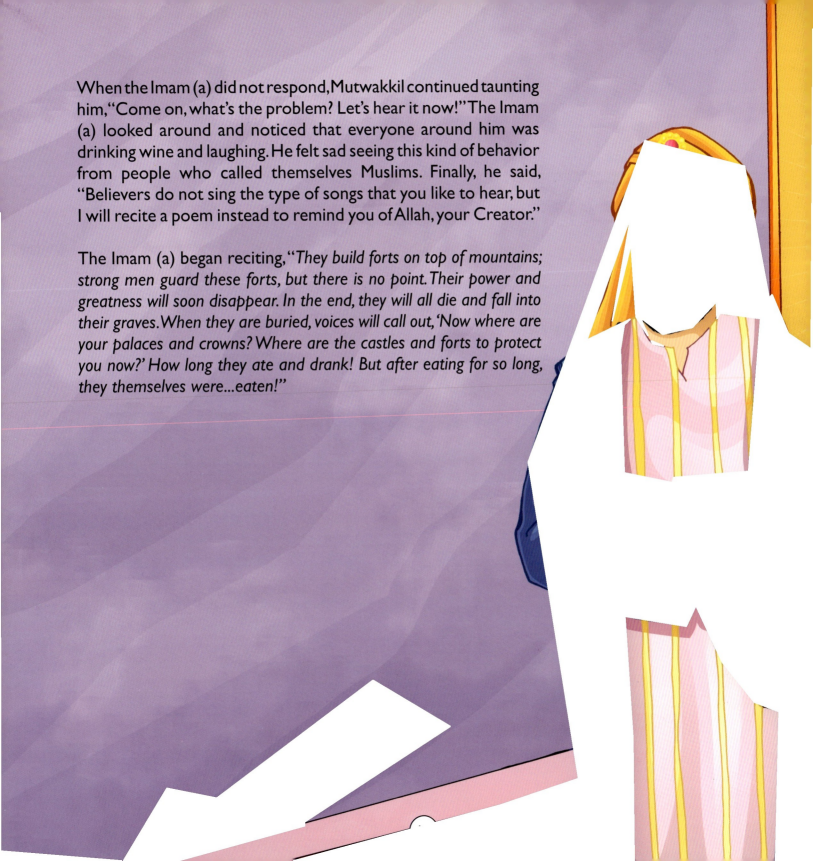

Everyone suddenly fell silent. Mutawakkil dropped his goblet, spilling his drink all over the carpet. His face turned pale and he was speechless. Moved by Imam al-Hadi's words, everyone around him began sobbing.

They felt very sorry for their actions. You see, the Imam (a) *guided* them by showing them what they were doing was wrong!

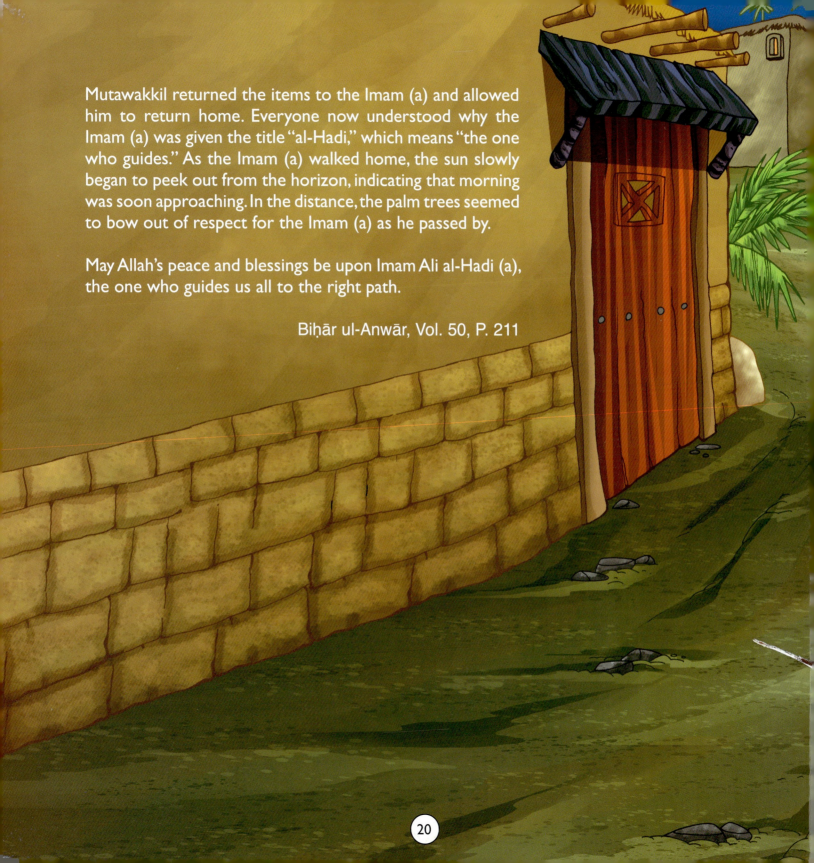

Mutawakkil returned the items to the Imam (a) and allowed him to return home. Everyone now understood why the Imam (a) was given the title "al-Hadi," which means "the one who guides." As the Imam (a) walked home, the sun slowly began to peek out from the horizon, indicating that morning was soon approaching. In the distance, the palm trees seemed to bow out of respect for the Imam (a) as he passed by.

May Allah's peace and blessings be upon Imam Ali al-Hadi (a), the one who guides us all to the right path.

Biḥār ul-Anwār, Vol. 50, P. 211